LAO
BASICS

T0151913

Sam Brier is the owner of Academic Experiences Abroad (www.AEA-Asia.com), which specializes in customized educational programs to Asia. Part of the proceeds from this book go toward AEA scholarships. Sam is also the author of *Instant Vietnamese* (Tuttle Publishing). Sam and his wife, Linh, live in Portland, Oregon.

LAO
BASICS

An Introduction to the Lao Language

Sam Brier

TUTTLE Publishing

Tokyo | Rutland, Vermont | Singapore

THE TUTTLE STORY

"Books to Span the East and West"

Our core mission at Tuttle Publishing is to create books which bring people together one page at a time. Tuttle was founded in 1832 in the small New England town of Rutland, Vermont (USA). Our fundamental values remain as strong today as they were then—to publish best-in-class books informing the English-speaking world about the countries and peoples of Asia. The world has become a smaller place today and Asia's economic, cultural and political influence has expanded, yet the need for meaningful dialogue and information about this diverse region has never been greater. Since 1948, Tuttle has been a leader in publishing books on the cultures, arts, cuisines, languages and literatures of Asia. Our authors and photographers have won numerous awards and Tuttle has published thousands of books on subjects ranging from martial arts to paper crafts. We welcome you to explore the wealth of information available on Asia at www.tuttlepublishing.com.

Published by Tuttle Publishing, an imprint of Periplus Editions (HK) Ltd.

Copyright © 2010 Periplus Editions (HK) Ltd.

Cover photo: © 0tvalo. Dreamstime. com. The Pha That Luang monument in Vientiane, Laos.

Library of Congress Cataloging Number: 2009933399

ISBN 978-0-8048-4099-6

First edition
23 22 21 20   5 4 3 2   2002MP
Printed in Singapore

Distributed by

North America, Latin America & Europe
Tuttle Publishing
364 Innovation Drive
North Clarendon
VT 05759-9436 U.S.A.
Tel: 1 (802) 773-8930
Fax: 1 (802) 773-6993
info@tuttlepublishing.com
www.tuttlepublishing.com

Asia Pacific
Berkeley Books Pte. Ltd.
3 Kallang Sector #04-01
Singapore 349278
Tel: (65) 6741-2178
Fax: (65) 6741-2179
inquiries@periplus.com.sg
www.periplus.com

Contents

Acknowledgments

Although this is a short book, many thanks are in order:

Thank you Gordon Allison, the author of *Easy Thai*—the book that *Lao Basics* is modeled after. I found *Easy Thai* in a Bangkok bookstore and quickly saw that it simplified what seemed to me a very complex language. After using it to grasp the basics of Thai in a rather short period of time, I thought to myself, "If there were only a book like this for learning Lao." Unable to find one, I decided to write it myself.

Back in Lao, I asked Tee to be my co-author, and thankfully she accepted. Tee pushed *Lao Basics* through its most difficult phase—the first draft. Souphing Saphakdy edited it to this final version. Without either of them, this book would not be in your hands now. We hope that *Lao Basics* survives the test of time, as has Allison's *Easy Thai*, first printed in 1968 and still widely available after more than 27 printings.

There are also the many others I met in Lao who made me want to stay longer than I had planned. Much longer. And I did. Their names, if I knew half of them, would double the size of this book. Some of them I can't forget, however: Simon Creak, Leisa Tyler, Carrie-Anne Best, Clif Meys, Liam Thammavongsa, Manichanh (Lang) Sichanhthapadid, Rome, Alain, Nick, the entire staff of the U.S. Embassy, plus Ely Ruel and everyone else at the Vientiane International School.

Although I didn't know my wife, Linh, when I started this project, it wouldn't feel right if I didn't thank her for supporting me since the day we met. It would be akin to not thanking my parents, who never thought I'd live in Asia so many years, but have come to visit many times. Thank you.

Even with a great co-author, editor and excellent friends, plus the inspiration, energy and support to finish a book, it takes something special to bring it to market. Some might call it luck, but I call it a publisher. The hardest part in the publishing process is not necessarily finding a publisher, however; it's finding the right publisher, and I have been fortunate enough to find Tuttle Publishing and Sandra Korinchak, my editor, who have been wonderful to work with on this and our other projects together so far: *A Chinese Phrase a Day Practice Pad* and *A Japanese Phrase a Day Practice Pad*.

Finally, I'd like to thank you for having an interest in Lao, a language spoken by relatively few, but more than worth the effort to learn.

Introduction

Why *Lao Basics?*

Some readers may wonder why this book is not called *Laotian Basics*, or perhaps even *Laos Basics*. The English words *Laos* and *Laotian* are derived from the Lao language, but they are not accurate transliterations. The French added the "s" to *Lao*, which is the correct pronunciation of the country as well as the language and the people. For example: "Lao people speak Lao in Lao." Hence, we have called this book *Lao Basics*.

Lao Basics teaches conversational Lao from the very beginning with an emphasis on reading and writing. It follows the same simple, effective learning format as *Easy Thai* by Gordon Allison, which has remained popular and in print since its publication in 1968.

Students of Thai will find Lao quite simple, as much of these two languages are the same or very similar. Likewise, after learning Lao, Thai (with a more complex alphabet) will be much easier to study. These languages derive from Sanskrit and share many of the same consonants, vowels, vocabulary and grammar. A Thai speaker learning Lao would be comparable to a French speaker studying Italian or vice versa.

Lao Basics is organized so that you will first learn to read, write, speak and comprehend the 26 consonants in their tonal classes. Once you have mastered these, you will study the 28 vowels in subsets. Within each vowel grouping, you will learn vocabulary, conversational phrases, alphabetical order and sentence structure through exercises that grow more challenging as your vocabulary increases.

As you progress through *Lao Basics*, vocabulary from previous lessons will be repeated regularly and your command of the written and spoken language will steadily improve.

And you can do all of this on your own. Each chapter's Lao words and exercises have been recorded on the accompanying CD, and all of the exercise answers are in the back of the book.

How to Use This Book

The Lao alphabet may look formidable, but it contains clear rules, which make learning to read and spell in Lao much easier than in English. For example, consonants and vowels are read as they are written and vice versa, as in Spanish; i.e., pronunciation does not change. And even though vowel placement may look confusing to the novice, vowels do not change location. The logical design of the written language greatly helps to learn the spoken language, and *Lao Basics* takes advantage of this in its layout.

In *Lao Basics*, the 26 Lao consonants are broken down into three classes rather than taught in alphabetical order. This follows the traditional teaching format of Lao, and we also follow this method because each grouping references a tonal category.

To use *Lao Basics* effectively, plan to move on to the next chapter only after you are confident that you have mastered the previous one. Practice writing each letter as you say it until you are 75% sure that you can recognize, say and write each correctly from memory; then move on to the exercises for reinforcement. And don't forget to listen to the audio CD for correct pronunciation. The answers to all exercises are at the back of the book.

Like English, Lao is read left to right and follows the Subject-Verb-Object word order. Additionally, most Lao letters are pronounced just like sounds that exist in English.

Lao differs from English in other ways, however. Lao has relatively little grammar, no plurals, few articles, and regularly leaves out the subject pronoun (I, He, She...) at the beginning of sentences when the context is understood. In this sense Lao can be much easier to learn than other languages.

Other aspects are more difficult to get used to. For example, there are no spaces between words in the written language; a special word is added to the end of sentences (**baw**), rather than inflection, that turns statements into questions; some vowel sounds are unfamiliar to the English speaker, and certain vowels are placed to the left of consonants, while other vowels are placed to the right, above and below. But, have no fear—unlike English, the rules are easy to follow, and each vowel combination is only pronounced one way.

A note on writing Lao script: Most consonants and some vowels start with a small loop. In order to write the letter correctly, *start with the loop at one end of the letter* and follow the letter through to the other end. Here is an example:

Start

Each chapter contains explanations where necessary to make your learning experience more enjoyable, so let's leave it at that and get started.

The Tones

Consonant/Tonal Groupings

This chapter gives a brief overview of the Lao tones, and we recommend that you work with both the accompanying audio CD and a Lao language teacher to master them.

Lao Basics divides each consonant into one of the three traditional groupings (or classes): Mid, Low, or High. The consonants in each particular grouping follow the same rules when accompanied by various combinations of ending consonants, vowels (short, long or nasal), and tonal marks. For example, all eight Mid consonants follow the same rules, whereas Low consonants have their own rules. And High consonants have their own rules. Sometimes, rules do overlap groups, but rules rarely cover all groups.

It can be very difficult to memorize a chart with all of these peculiarities, and for that reason *Lao Basics* takes a different path. **Instead of memorizing a chart, you will learn to read, write, comprehend and say each consonant, each vowel, each word and each sentence in this book; in short you will learn by doing.**

Listen closely to the pronunciation on the CD, and if possible, work with a native Lao speaker to master these sounds.

Tone Marks

There are four tonal marks that are placed over some Lao vowels from time to time, but only two are regularly used, and we have attempted to teach you mostly words without tone marks for the first part of the vowel section.

The first tonal symbol is called **mai eik** (pronounced "my ehk"). It looks like a short number "1" placed over a letter ['] and causes the sound of all words that contain this tone mark to take on a middle (slightly high) pitch. Here are some examples:

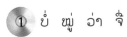

The second tonal symbol is called **mai too**. You will learn later in the vowel section that **mai** is a short sound and **too** is a long sound, pronounced "my toe." Since English is rarely consistent in pronunciation, however, we use a different transliteration system, which you will learn as you progress through the book. **Mai too** looks like a tiny, squiggly number "2" with a long tail [ˇ]. When this is placed over a vowel, it causes the sound of Mid and Low Consonant words to drop from a high tone to a low one, while it causes words starting with a High consonant to fall from an already low starting point. Here are some examples:

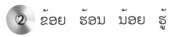

The third tonal symbol is **mai jat dta waa** or "my jaht dtah wah" [˜] and the fourth is **mai dtii** or "my dtee" [˙]. The former looks like a little lowercase *m* with a tail, and the latter looks like a tiny plus sign. They are both seldom used and change the sound of words to a short "pop"ping sound.

The Consonants

LESSON 1

Mid Consonants (Part I)

LAO LETTER	ALPHABETICAL ORDER	ENGLISH PHONETICS	ENGLISH SOUND
ກ	1	gaw	*g*
ຈ	5	jaw	*j*
ດ	9	daw	*d*
ຕ	10	dtaw	*dt*

The letter **ກ** is often transliterated as *k* in other Lao language books instead of *g*, as we have used here. When found at the *beginning* of a word, the American *g* sound is spot-on, but a soft *k* sound is appropriate when **ກ** is found at the *end* of a word. An easy way to remember this is that *g* comes before *k* in the English alphabet.

The sound **aw** is added to Lao letters to make the name of the letter. For example, instead of saying **gee** as we would for the letter *g* in English, one must say **gaw** for the letter **ກ**, as shown in the chart.

There are no capital or lowercase letters in Lao, and there are no spaces between words in sentences.

As you look at each Lao example and listen to the audio, below and throughout these chapters, focus on hearing the consonant's sound; don't worry about understanding entire words.

Examples of **ກ** sound at the beginning of a word: ກັບ / ກິນ
Examples of **ກ** sound at the end of a word: ນົກ / ຮັກ

The letter **ຈ** is often written as *ch* in other guides (often printed in England), but once again you will find that the American English *j* is more accurate.

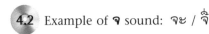

4.2 Example of ** จ** sound: จะ / จิ้

The letter **ด** at the beginning of a word sounds like an American **d**, with the **tongue curved farther back toward the center of the roof of the mouth**. At the end of a word, **ด** has the sound of a soft **t**.

4.3 Examples of **ด** sound at the beginning of a word: ดาว / ดิ
Examples of **ด** sound at the end of a word: ปิด / ยุด

The letter **ต** has no exact mirror sound in English, but does come close to the soft **t** spoken at the end of English words. For example: the soft **t** in *what*, but not the **t** in *Texas*. It is therefore not the equivalent of a plain **t** as it is so often written. It is rather a mix between a **d** and **t**, hence **dt**. This sound is made by slightly touching your **tongue against the back of your upper-front teeth** and making a **d** sound. These fine subtleties may not sound much different to you and me, but they do change the meaning for Lao people.

4.4 Examples of **ต** sound: ต๋อะ / แตๆ

Exercises

Refer to the answer key at the back of the book when necessary. If you need to refer to the answer key during this first exercise you probably haven't spent enough time writing each letter and memorizing the chart.

A. Write in English:

1.	ด	6.	ด
2.	จ	7.	ๆ
3.	ๆ	8.	จ
4.	ต	9.	ต
5.	จ	10.	ๆ

5.1 Now listen to these letters, pronounced on the CD. Repeat each one several times to practice.

B. Write in Lao:

1. daw
2. gaw
3. dtaw
4. jaw
5. dtaw

6. gaw
7. jaw
8. dtaw
9. daw
10. gaw

Now listen to these letters, pronounced on the CD. Repeat each one several times to practice.

LESSON 2

Mid Consonants (Part II)

LAO LETTER	ALPHABETICAL ORDER	ENGLISH PHONETICS	ENGLISH SOUND
ບ	14	baw	*b*
ປ	15	bpaw	*bp*
ຍ	21	yaw	*y*
ອ	32	aw	*aw*

The letter **ບ** sounds like an American **b** at the beginning of a word, but a soft American **p** at the end of a word.

Examples of **ບ** sound at the beginning of a word: ບໍ່ / ບອກ

Examples of **ບ** sound at the end of a word: ກັບ / ແຂບ

The letter **ປ** has no exact English counterpart and it is not a **p** as is so often written. Instead it is a **b** unaspirated (no air leaves your mouth) with a slight **p** sound included; hence use **bp**. This sound can be made by putting your lips together like you are going to say a **b** and then pushing your lips with a bit of air like you are saying a soft **p** sound (but do not let air out). It is not usually mastered too quickly and may require much practice. If you get frustrated with this sound, say the sound **p**, and most people will understand what you are saying.

Examples of **ປ** sound: ປິດ / ປາ

The letter **ອ** has the audacity to act as a vowel, although it is included with the consonants. When accompanied by consonants, it sounds like **aw** (**aw**kward); when combined only with a vowel it takes on that vowel's sound. For now, however, we will only focus on its use with consonants and will study how it works with vowels when we reach that section.

3 Examples of **ອ** sound when combined with a consonant: ຂອງ / ບອກ

Exercises

A. Write in English:

1.	ດ	9.	ຕ
2.	ຈ	10.	ປ
3.	ຕ	11.	ຈ
4.	ຍ	12.	ອ
5.	ອ	13.	ບ
6.	ປ	14.	ຍ
7.	ບ	15.	ກ
8.	ອ	16.	ດ

Now listen to these letters, pronounced on the CD.
Repeat each one several times to practice.

B. Write in Lao:

1.	aw	9.	gaw
2.	yaw	10.	daw
3.	bpaw	11.	aw
4.	dtaw	12.	jaw
5.	gaw	13.	bpaw
6.	aw	14.	daw
7.	jaw	15.	yaw
8.	baw	16.	aw

Now listen to these letters, pronounced on the CD.
Repeat each one several times to practice.

LESSON 3
Low Consonants (Part I)

LAO LETTER	ALPHABETICAL ORDER	ENGLISH PHONETICS	ENGLISH SOUND
ກ	3	kaw	*k*
ງ	4	ngaw	*ng*
ຊ	7	saw	*s*
ຍ	8	nyaw	*ny*
ທ	12	taw	*t*
ນ	13	naw	*n*

Found at the beginning and end of words, **ງ** is spoken just like the *ng* in *sing*. **Native English speakers will have no problem correctly pronouncing** *ng* **at the end of words, but it can be difficult to grasp when spoken first.** As the back of your tongue hits the top-back of the roof of your mouth, on the edge of your throat, your nose will vibrate a bit when you try to say the *ng* in *sing* without the *si*. The sound comes out of both your nose and mouth; i.e., you can't say it properly if you pinch your nose closed. One way to practice this sound is to say *Sing it* over and over, eventually getting to the point where you can remove the *s* and then the *i* from *sing*. Then you will be saying **ngit**, which is a good start.

Examples of **ງ** sound at the beginning of a word: ງົວ / ເງິນ
Examples of **ງ** sound at the end of a word: ເຄື່ອງ / ສ]ງ

The letter **ຍ** at the *beginning* of a word sounds like **nyuh** or like the **nio** in *onion*, but is pronounced like the *y* in *boy* at the *end* of a word.

Examples of **ຍ** sound at the beginning of a word: ຍັງ / ຍຸງ
Examples of **ຍ** sound at the end of a word: ເຄືຍ / ນອຍ

Exercises

A. Write in English:

1. ດ	9. ຊ	17. ຄ
2. ຊ	10. ຕ	18. ຢ
3. ກ	11. ຈ	19. ບ
4. ງ	12. ດ	20. ຕ
5. ປ	13. ນ	21. ກ
6. ຈ	14. ງ	22. ອ
7. ຍ	15. ບ	23. ນ
8. ຄ	16. ປ	24. ຊ

Now listen to these letters, pronounced on the CD.
Repeat each one several times to practice.

B. Write in Lao:

1. kaw	9. nyaw	17. saw
2. daw	10. bpaw	18. gaw
3. ngaw	11. taw	19. naw
4. saw	12. aw	20. bpaw
5. naw	13. yaw	21. ngaw
6. baw	14. daw	22. baw
7. dtaw	15. jaw	23. kaw
8. ngaw	16. kaw	24. daw

Now listen to these letters, pronounced on the CD.
Repeat each one several times to practice.

LESSON 4

Low Consonants (Part II)

LAO LETTER	ALPHABETICAL ORDER	ENGLISH PHONETICS	ENGLISH SOUND
ຜ	18	paw	*p*
ຝ	19	faw	*f*
ມ	20	maw	*m*
ລ	22	law	*l*
ວ	23	waw	*w*
ຣ	32	haw	*h*

ວ (**waw**) acts both as a consonant and vowel, which you will see later. Some language guides classify this sound as *v* and some as *w*, and sometimes it is hard to tell which it is when it begins a word. For clarity's sake we have chosen *w*, since it is quite clear that Lao people do say "wolleyball" rather than "volleyball." When placed at the end of a word, like ລາວ (*Lao*), ວ sounds like "oh" and is transliterated as the *o* in *Lao*. (Although some might feel that it sounds closer to the *ow* in *now*, the *ow* is used for another vowel sound.)

Examples of ວ sound at the beginning of a word: ວຽກ / ເວລາ
Examples of ວ sound at the end of a word: ລາວ / ດາວ

Note: You will see in the vowel section that *Lao* would normally be written as *Laao* using our transliteration system, but because it is so commonly written in English as "Lao," we have opted to simply leave it be when we use it as an English word. Remember, however, that *Lao* is a long sound (*laao*).

Before 1975, the Lao language did have the letter ຣ (**raw**), which looks quite similar to the ຮ (**haw**), except that the *r* is rounded at the top while the *h* is bent upward in the same place. It is worth noting this in case you study Thai or visit Thailand, where the *r* is still in use and regularly replaces the Lao *h* sound in words such as **hoong hian** (*school*). In Thai, it is **roong rian**.

2 Example of ຣ sound: ໂຣງຮຽນ

Exercises

A. Write in English:

15 1. ຜ   11. ຄ   21. ດ

2. ບ   12. ຈ   22. ລ

3. ທ   13. ຕ   23. ຍ

4. ດ   14. ຊ   24. ຮ

5. ພ   15. ນ   25. ມ

6. ວ   16. ຍ   26. ຜ

7. ລ   17. ທ   27. ທ

8. ບ   16 18. ວ   28. ອ

9. ຮ   19. ງ   29. ບ

10. ພ   20. ກ   30. ດ

Now listen to these letters, pronounced on the CD.
Repeat each one several times to practice.

B. Write the English for the Lao script:

1. daw	11. baw	21. dtaw
2. paw	12. dtaw	22. kaw
3. law	13. maw	23. naw
4. maw	14. waw	24. bpaw
5. naw	15. faw	25. waw
6. aw	16. yaw	26. ngaw
7. saw	17. nyaw	27. yaw
8. jaw	18. saw	28. gaw
9. faw	19. ngaw	29. nyaw
10. paw	20. taw	30. faw

 Now listen to these letters, pronounced on the CD.
Repeat each one several times to practice.

LESSON 5

High Consonants

LAO LETTER	ALPHABETICAL ORDER	ENGLISH PHONETICS	ENGLISH SOUND
ຂ	2	k(h)aw	*(h)*
ສ	6	saw	*s*
ຖ	11	t(h)aw	*t(h)*
ຜ	16	p(h)aw	*p(h)*
ຝ	17	faw	*f*
ຫ	24	haw	*h*

The transliterated *(h)* that you will see from here on out means there is a slight aspiration (puff of air) after the initial letter. It's natural for English speakers to aspirate words unknowingly, such as *park, boy*, and *huh?* The letters we aspirate are not always the same in Lao, however. Pay close attention to these, as some look and sound quite similar, such as ຜ *(p)* and ຜ *(ph)*.

Examples of ຜ sound: ແຜງ / ສຸພາບ
Examples of ຜ sound: ຜົວ / ຜູ້ສາວ

Exercises

A. Write in English:

1. ຜ	6. ດ	11. ລ
2. ບ	7. ຝ	12. ບ
3. ຂ	8. ວ	13. ຣ
4. ມ	9. ສ	14. ຜ
5. ຫ	10. ຫ	15. ຫ

16. ພ	25. ວ	34. ມ
17. ຄ	26. ງ	35. ຜ
18. ຈ	27. ຫ	36. ຜ
19. ຕ	28. ກ	37. ຫ
20. ຊ	29. ດ	38. ອ
21. ບ	30. ລ	39. ປ
22. ຍ	31. ຢ	40. ຫ
23. ຫ	32. ຂ	
24. ຖ	33. ຮ	

Now listen to these letters, pronounced on the CD.
Repeat each one several times to practice.

B. Write in Lao:

1. daw	15. faw	29. nyaw
2. paw	16. yaw	30. faw
3. law	17. nyaw	31. haw
4. maw	18. saw	32. jaw
5. naw	19. ngaw	33. maw
6. aw	20. taw	34. p(h)aw
7. haw	21. dtaw	35. paw
8. jaw	22. k(h)aw	36. law
9. t(h)aw	23. naw	37. faw
10. p(h)aw	24. bpaw	38. dtaw
11. baw	25. waw	39. saw
12. kaw	26. ngaw	40. naw
13. maw	27. yaw	
14. waw	28. gaw	

Note: Don't forget—there are now two ways to write the Lao *s*, *f* and *h*.

Now listen to these letters, pronounced on the CD.

Repeat each one several times to practice.

You've finished learning the 26 Lao consonants. Now, there are just six special spellings to learn. **They are grouped along with the Rising Consonants** you just studied, but we are giving them their own special section so you don't get overloaded.

LESSON 6

High Consonants with Special Spellings

23

LAO LETTER	ALPHABETICAL ORDER	ENGLISH PHONETICS	ENGLISH SOUND
ຫງ	26	ngaw	*ng*
ຫຍ	27	nyaw	*ny*
ໜ	28	naw	*n*
ໝ	29	maw	*m*
ຫຼ or ຫລ	30	law	*l*
ຫວ	31	waw	*w*

The letter ຫ (**haw**) is added to the other letters only for some words, but the word maintains the sound of the second letter.

ໜ and ໝ are created like this: ຫ + ນ = ໜ
ຫ + ມ = ໝ

Exercises

A. Write in English:

24
1. ຫ	10. ຍ	19. ຫວ
2. ຕ	11. ລ	20. ຫລ
3. ສ	12. ໝ	21. ປ
4. ຊ	13. ຈ	22. ຜ
5. ພ	14. ໜ	23. ບ
6. ຫຍ	15. ຖ	24. ຫຼ
7. ກ	16. ຂ	25. ວ
8. ມ	17. ຕ	26. ຢ
9. ນ	**25** 18. ດ	27. ຫງ

28. ມ	37. ກ	46. ຢ
29. ອ	38. ທ	47. ຫ
30. ຣ	39. ຫລ	48. ດ
31. ຕ	40. ບ	49. ຕ
32. ງ	41. ຍ	50. ຫຍ
33. ໝ	42. ປ	51. ຊ
34. ຖ	43. ຣ	52. ໝ
35. ສ	44. ພ	
36. ດ	45. ຍ	

Now listen to these letters, pronounced on the CD.

Repeat each one several times to practice.

B. Write in Lao:

Note: There are two ways to write the characters you just learned: with and without the ຫ.

26
1. daw
2. k(h)aw
3. waw
4. paw
5. taw
6. saw
7. yaw
8. haw
9. law
10. jaw
11. dtaw
12. faw
13. aw
14. gaw
15. k(h)aw
16. baw
17. maw
18. naw

27
19. bpaw
20. faw
21. t(h)aw
22. nyaw
23. ngaw
24. p(h)aw
25. law
26. saw
27. taw
28. dtaw
29. bpaw
30. yaw
31. gaw
32. kaw
33. naw
34. jaw
35. taw
36. waw

28
37. haw
38. nyaw
39. paw
40. yaw
41. maw
42. daw
43. aw
44. t(h)aw
45. faw
46. ngaw
47. p(h)aw
48. law
49. baw
50. bpaw
51. daw
52. maw

Now listen to these letters, pronounced on the CD. You'll notice that in cases where there are two spellings, the audio states both, as they are spoken slightly differently.

Repeat each one several times to practice.

REVIEW 1
LESSON 7

Alphabetical Order of Consonants as Found in Dictionary:

1.	ກ	17.	ຜ
2.	ຂ	18.	ພ
3.	ຄ	19.	ຟ
4.	ງ	20.	ມ
5.	ຈ	21.	ຍ
6.	ສ	22.	ລ
7.	ຊ	23.	ວ
8.	ຢ	24.	ຫ
9.	ດ	25.	ອ
10.	ຕ	26.	ຮ
11.	ຖ	27.	ຫງ
12.	ທ	28.	ຫຍ
13.	ນ	29.	ໜ
14.	ບ	30.	ໝ
15.	ປ	31.	ຫຼ / ຫລ
16.	ຜ	32.	ຫວ

The Vowels

LESSON 8

Right Side Vowels

LAO LETTER	ALPHABETICAL ORDER	ENGLISH SOUND	ENGLISH SPELLING
Xະ	1	as in *ha!* (short)	*a*
Xາ	3	as in *father* (long)	*aa*
X̊ າ	32	as in U.S. *Mom* (long)	*aam*

Examples of Xະ sound: ຈະ, ຕະ, ບະ
Examples of Xາ sound: ປາ, ມາ, ທາກ
Examples of X̊ າ sound: ບໍາ, ດໍາ, ທໍາ

The construction of Lao words, with the above vowels, is shown below:

Ex. ຈ + xະ = ຈະ
   J + *a* = Ja

Ex. ມ + xາ = ມາ
   M + *aa* = Maa

Ex. ດ + x̊ າ = ດໍາ
   D + *aam* = Daam

Notice that Lao has "short" and "long" vowel sounds. It is important to pay attention to this point in words that you learn, because meanings do vary accordingly.

The vowel x̊ າ is made up of two separate vowel parts: X̊ and Xາ. You'll learn more about these soon.

Exercises

A. Write in English:

1.	ຈະ	8.	ປາ	15.	ຖາມ
2.	ມາ	9.	ລາວ	16.	ທຳລາຍ
3.	ນ້ຳ	10.	ງາມ	17.	ທາກ
4.	ຢາ	11.	ດຳ	18.	ຕະຫຼາດ
5.	ຕາ	12.	ຂາ	19.	ຢາກ
6.	ຕາຍ	13.	ຍາກ	20.	ຂາວ
7.	ຢາກ	14.	ດາວ		

 Now listen to these words, pronounced on the CD.
Repeat each one several times to practice.

B. Write in Lao:

1.	daao	8.	yaa	15.	dtalaat
2.	laao	9.	naam	16.	daam
3.	ngaam	10.	yaak	17.	bpaa
4.	ja	11.	haak	18.	saa
5.	yaak	12.	k(h)aao	19.	maa
6.	nyaak	13.	naam	20.	dtaai
7.	t(h)aam	14.	laao		

 Now listen to these words, pronounced on the CD.
Repeat each one several times to practice.

C. Put the following words in alphabetical order:

1. ລາວ, ຂາ, ຈະ, ທາກ
2. ຢາກ, ຕາ, ຢາ, ງາມ, ຕະຫຼາດ, ດາວ
3. ຂາວ, ປາ, ຕາ, ນ້ຳ ຖາມ, ຢາກ, ຕາຍ, ດາວ, ລາວ

LESSON 9
Vocabulary A

Some of the words you just learned to read and write, along with a few new ones, are listed in alphabetical order below with their meanings.

#	LAO	ENGLISH	TRANSLATION(S)
1	ຂາວ	k(h)aao	white (*adj*)
2	ລາວ	laao	(s)he (*n*), Laos (*n*)
3	ງາມ	ngaam	pretty (*adj*)
4	ຈະ	ja	will (*in the future*)
5	ຊາ	saa	tea (*n*)
6	(ຊອກ)ຫາ	(sawk) haa	look for (*v*)
7	ຍາກ	nyaak	difficult (*adj*)
8	ດາວ	daao	star in sky (*n*), person's name
9	ຕະຫຼາດ	dtalaat	market (*n*)
10	ຖາມ	t(h)aam	ask (*v*)
11	ນ້ຳ	naam	water (*n*)
12	ປາ	bpaa	fish (*n*)
13	ມາ	maa	come (*v*)
14	ຢາ	yaa	medicine (*n*)
15	ຢາກ	yaak	want (*v*)
16	ຮາກ	haak	vomit (*n*), (*v*)

Nouns and verbs do not change form in Lao. In other words, *come* and *came* are both the same word: ມາ (**maa**). Other words are added in Lao to give time/ tense context. This will be explained in more detail further on.

Articles that we are familiar with in English, such as a, *an*, *the*, are not used in Lao, but other words are used to signify superlatives and the kinds of objects you are counting (round, flat, animal, person, etc.).

ຢາກ (**yaak**) means *to want*. When a <u>verb</u> follows, it means you <u>*want to do*</u> something. When you want an object, say "**Yaak dai** [object]."

Exercises

A. Translate into English:

1. ຢາດາວ
2. ປາງາມ
3. ດາວຊອກທາຊາ
4. ລາວຮາກ

5. ລາວຢາກມາຕະຫຼາດ
6. ດາວມາ
7. ປາຊາວ
8. ລາວຈະຊອກທາປາ

 Now listen to these phrases, pronounced on the CD.
Repeat each one several times to practice.

B. Translate into Lao:

1. White fish.
2. Dao is looking for medicine.
3. It's difficult.
4. (S)he vomited.

5. The fish will come.
6. Dao's tea.
7. She is pretty.
8. The fish wants to vomit.

Now listen to these phrases, pronounced on the CD.
Repeat each one several times to practice.

Notes:

Adjectives follow their respective nouns. For example, "black car" in English becomes "car black" in Lao.

Possessives work like this: "Sam's dog" in English becomes "dog (of) Sam" in Lao, but the *of* is often left out. This will be explained in more detail when we learn about the word for *of*.

LESSON 10

Top Vowels

LAO LETTER	ALPHABETICAL ORDER	ENGLISH SOUND	ENGLISH SPELLING
x̆x	2	as in *ah!* (short) same as xະ	*a*
x̂x	17	as in home	*o*
X̆	4	as in *it* (short)	*i*
X̂	5	as in b*ee* (*long*)	*ii*
X̆	6	as in l*oo*k (short)	*uh*
X̂	7	as in l*oo*k (long)	*uhh*
X̊	20	as in l*aw*	*aw*

Examples of x̆x sound: ກັບ, ຮັກ, ຍັງ
Examples of x̂x sound: ຄົນ, ທົກ, ນົກ
Examples of X̆ sound: ປິດ, ກິນ
Examples of X̂ sound: ມີ, ດີ
Examples of X̆ sound: ຂຶມ, ສຶ
Examples of X̂ sound: ລືມ, ຈື່, ຄືກັນ
Examples of X̊ sound: ຂໍ, ບໍ່

The construction of Lao words, with the above vowels, is shown below:

Ex. ກ + ◌ັ + ບ = ກັບ
   g + *a* + *p* = gap

Ex. ຄ + ◌ົ + ນ = ຄົນ
   k + *o* + *n* = kon

Ex. ປ + ◌ິ + ດ = ປິດ
   bp + *i* + *t* = bpit

Ex. ມ + ◌ີ = ມີ
   m + *ii* = mii

Ex. ຂ + ◌ຶ + ມ = ຂຶມ
   k(h) + *uh* + *m* = k(h)uhm

Ex. ລ + ◌ື + ມ = ລືມ
   l + *uhh* + *m* = luhhm

Ex. ຂ + ◌ໍ = ຂໍ
   k(h) + *aw* = k(h)aw

Exercises

A. Write in English:

1.	ດິຫຼາຍ	8.	ຣັກ	15.	ຍັງ
2.	ກັບ	9.	ຫຼື	16.	ບໍ່
3.	ຈຸ	10.	ທິກ	17.	ຖຶກ
4.	ຂໍ	11.	ບໍ	18.	ຄິກັບ
5.	ມີ	12.	ທຳມະດາໆ	19.	ນິກ
6.	ປິດ	13.	ຄົນລາວ	20.	ທັຍໆ
7.	ກິນ	14.	ລືມ		

38 Now listen to these words/phrases, pronounced on the CD. Repeat each one several times to practice.

B. Write in Lao:

1.	mii	11.	t(h)uhhk
2.	luhhm	12.	hak
3.	kuhhn	13.	nok
4.	dii laai	14.	gin
5.	baw	15.	kuhh gan
6.	nyang	16.	tam ma daa
7.	yaa	17.	juhh
8.	bpit	18.	gap
9.	k(h)aw	19.	kon laao
10.	hok	20.	baw

39 Now listen to these words/phrases, pronounced on the CD. Repeat each one several times to practice.

C. Put the following words in alphabetical order:

1. ນົກ, ກັບ, ທຳມະດາ, ລົມ
2. ຈຸ່, ຂໍ, ມິ, ປິດ, ກັບ, ບໍ່, ຄົນລາວ, ກິນ
3. ຄືກັນ, ຮັກ, ຫູ້, ກິນ, ຍັງ, ບໍ່, ຂໍ, ດິຫງາຍ

LESSON 11

Vocabulary B

#	LAO	ENGLISH	TRANSLATION(S)
1	ກັບ(ບ້ານ)	gap(baan)	with, return (home) (v), (n)
2	ກິນ	gin	eat (v)
3	ຂໍ	k(h)aw	may (used when asking for something)
4	ຄືກັນ	kuhh'gan	same, also (adj)
5	ຄົນລາວ	kon laao	Lao person (n)
6	ຈື່	juhh	remember (v)
7	ຍັງ	nyang	not yet (adv)
8	ດີຫຼາຍ	dii laai	very good (adv, adj)
9	ທຳມະດາ	tam ma daa	normal, regular (adj)
10	ນົກ	nok	bird, person's name (n)
11	ບໍ່	baw	no, ?
12	ປິດ	bpit	close (v)
13	ມັກ	mak	like (v)
14	ມີ	mii	have (v)
15	ລືມ	luhhm	forget (v)
16	ຮັກ	hak	love (v)

ກັບ (**gap**) is often used in conjunction with a place you are going back to such as home (ກັບບ້ານ / **gap baan**). For example, someone might ask you where you're going: **jow pbai sai?** You can reply **gap baan** ("Returning home").

41.1 ກັບ **gap**
ເຈົ້າໄປໃສ? **jow pbai sai?**
ກັບບ້ານ **gap ban.**

ຂໍ (**k(h)aw**) is usually used to ask for something. For example, **k(h)aw bpaa daae** (May I have the fish, please?). **Daae** means "please."

41.2 ຂໍ **k(h)aw**
ຂໍປາແດ່ **k(h)aw bpaa daae?**

ຄືກັນ (**kuhh'gan**) is usually placed after a subject or verb, similar to how we use *too, also, either* and *neither* in English. For example, **k(h)awy kuhh'gan** means "Me, too." **k(h)awy** means "I" or "me."

41.3 ຄືກັນ **kuhh'gan**
ຂອຍຄືກັນ **k(h)awy kuhh'gan.**

ດີ (**dii**) means "good"; ຫຼາຍ (**laai**) means "very" or "really." These words are used as often as we use them in English. ຫຼາຍ is always placed *after* the adjective (meaning "very" _____) or noun (meaning "many" or "a lot of" _____). For example, **dii laai** means "very good," and **nok laai** means "a lot of birds."

42.1 ດີ **dii**
ດີຫຼາຍ **dii laai**
ນົກຫຼາຍ **nok laai**

42.2 ທຳມະດາ (**tam ma daa**) is used to describe something as "regular, normal," or "so-so." It can indicate, for instance, the kind of gasoline that you want. Or if something is "only okay," ທຳມະດາ is the perfect thing to say.

ບໍ່ (**baw**) has a tonal mark over it called **mai ehk**. It has been covered in the tones chapter. ບໍ່ carries with it two meanings:

1) When used at the beginning of a sentence, or alone, it means "No," or "Don't."

2) When placed at the end of a sentence, ບໍ່ turns the statement into a question. But note, ບໍ່ is not needed to make interrogative sentences when question words are used, such as "what?", "how many?", "who?", etc.

3 ບໍ່ **baw**

ບໍ່ກິນປາ **baw gin bpaa** = Don't eat fish.

ກິນປາ **gin bpaa** = Eat fish.

ກິນປາບໍ່? **gin bpaa baw?** = Do you eat fish?

ບໍ່ກິນປາບໍ່? **baw gin bpaa baw?** = You don't eat fish?

Exercises

A. Translate into English:

1. ລາວຍັງບໍ່ກັບມາລາວ
2. ດາວມີນົກ
3. ຄົນລາວມັກກິນປາ
4. ລືມຄືກັນ

5. ນົກຈະຊອກທາງປາ
6. ມັກບໍ່?
7. ດາວມີຢາດີຫຼາຍ

Now listen to these words/phrases, pronounced on the CD.
Repeat each one several times to practice.

B. Translate into Lao:

1. She likes white birds.
2. He has a lot of water.
3. (I will) come back to the market, too.
4. Do you love her/him?
5. (S)he doesn't have any.
6. Ask her.
7. The market still has pretty birds, white fish (and) very good medicine.

Now listen to these words/phrases, pronounced on the CD.
Repeat each one several times to practice.

LESSON 12

Bottom Vowels

LAO	ALPHABETICAL ORDER	ENGLISH SOUND	ENGLISH
ຂຸ	8	as in gl*u*e (short)	*u*
ຂູ	9	as in d*u*de (long)	*uu*

Examples of ຂຸ sound: ຢຸ, ກຸ້ງ

Examples of ຂູ sound: ຢູ່, ຮູ້

In Between Vowels

LAO	ALPHABETICAL ORDER	ENGLISH SOUND	ENGLISH
xອx	21	as in l*aw* (long)	*aw*
xJ x	27	as in the name *Ia*n (short)	*ia*

Examples of xອx sound: ຂອງ, ນອນ

Examples of xJ x sound: ຮຽນ, ວຽກ

Top and Right/Middle Vowels

LAO	ALPHABETICAL ORDER	ENGLISH SOUND	ENGLISH
xົວະ, xົວx (rare)	30, 31	as in **u + a** (short)	*ua*
xົວ, xວx	32, 33	as in **uu + a** (long)	*uua*

Example of xົວະ, xົວx sound: ຕົວະ

Examples of xົວ, xວx sound: ວິວ, ກ່ວາໆ

ອ (**aw**) and ວ (**uua**) are both consonants as well as vowels (learned earlier). ອ is pronounced **aw-** unless next to another vowel, when it takes on the sound of that vowel.

ອ **aw**

ວ **uua**

Examples of ອ next to another vowel: ອາ / ອັງກິດ

Remember, when ວ begins or ends a word, it sounds like **w**. But as a vowel, in the middle of a word, it sounds like a short or long (**u**)**ua**.

Example of *short* ວ sound in the middle of a word: ຕົວະ

Examples of *long* ວ sound in the middle of a word: ເບື່ອ / ຄວາຍ

Exercises

A. Write in English:

1. ກຸ້ງ

2. ວິວ

3. ສຸພາບ

4. ຂ່ວນ

5. ຂອງ

6. ນວນ

7. ກ່ວາໆ

8. ຣວນ

9. ຕົວະ

10. ກ່ວາ	17. ຍຸງ	24. ຂ້ອຍ
11. ສອນ	18. ໝູ່	25. ຮອນ
12. ບອກ	19. ສ່ງງ	26. ນ້ອຍ
13. ສູບ	20. ຍຸດ	27. ຮູ້
14. ຈອກ	21. ຜູ້ຂາຍ	28. ຜູ້ສາວ
15. ຄວາຍ	22. ຄງວ	
16. ວງກ	23. ຂວາ	

49 Now listen to these words/phrases, pronounced on the CD.
Repeat each one several times to practice.

B. Write in Lao:

1. p(h)uua	11. huu	21. k(h)awy
2. nawn	12. kuaay	22. p(h)uu saai
3. gung	13. k(h)awg	23. bawk
4. jawk	14. p(h)uu saao	24. hian
5. yut	15. hawn	25. diao
6. suup	16. nyung	26. siang
7. supaap	17. dtua	27. sawn
8. nguua	18. muu	28. nawy
9. wiak	19. k(h)ian	
10. k(h)uaa	20. guaa	

50 Now listen to these words/phrases, pronounced on the CD.
Repeat each one several times to practice.

C. Put the following words in alphabetical order:

1. ສຸພາບ, ຍຸດ, ຜູ້ສາວ, ຄວາຍ

2. ຈອກ, ກຸ້ງ, ຄງວ, ຂອງ, ໝູ່, ຜູ້ສາວ, ວງກ, ດິກ່ວາ

3. ສູບ, ສອນ, ຜົວ, ຮູ້, ບອກ, ຮງນ, ວິວ, ຍຸງ

LESSON 13
Vocabulary C

#	LAO	ENGLISH	TRANSLATION(S)
1	ກຸ້ງ	gung	shrimp (*n*)
2	ກ່ວາ	guaa	intensifier ("-er")
3	ຂອງ	k(h)awng	possessive "of"
4	ຂ້ອຍ	k(h)awy	I (*personal pronoun*)
5	ຂຽນ	k(h)ian	write (*v*)
6	ຄວາຍ	kuaay	water buffalo (*n*)
7	ງົວ	nguua	cow, beef (*n*)
8	ຈອກ	jawk	cup, glass (*n*)
9	ສູບ	suup	smoke (*v*)
10	ສຽງ	siang	sound (*n*)
11	ຍຸງ	nyung	mosquito (*n*)
12	ດຽວ	diao	only (*adj*)
13	ຕົວະ	dtua	lie (*v*)
14	ນ້ອຍ	nawy	little (*adj*), name (*person*)
15	ນອນ	nawn	sleep (*v*)
16	ບອກ	bawk	tell (*v*)
17	ຜູ້ສາວ	p(h)uu saao	woman (n)
18	ຜູ້ຊາຍ	p(h)uu saai	man (*n*)
19	ຜົວ	p(h)uua	husband (*n*)

20	ໝູ່	**muu**	friend (*n*)
21	ຍຸດ	**yut**	stop (*v*)
22	ວຽກ	**wiak**	work (*n*)
23	ຮູ້	**huu**	know (*v*)
24	ຮຽນ	**hian**	study (*v*)
25	ຮ້ອນ	**hawn**	hot (*adj*)

ຂອງ (**k(h)awng**) is commonly left out of daily speech but is used often enough to learn. For example, "I" is ຂອຍ (**k(h)awy**), but "my" or "mine" is ຂອງຂອຍ. In other words, "of I" or "of me." Although Lao people may not use ຂອງ often, it may help you make yourself understood more clearly.

Suppose you're at a bar and you're not sure which drink is yours. You may point to a glass and ask, "ຂອງຂອຍບໍ?" **k(h)awng k(ha)wy baw?** (Is it mine?) And the person you're asking may very well say, "ຂອງຂອຍ." **k(h)awng k(h)awy**. (It's mine.) Or (s)he may say **baw huu**, "(I) don't know." Note that the subject, *glass* in this case, is usually left out if it is understood.

You'll see a few water buffaloes in Laos, but not as many as before. Remember, ຂໍ (**k(h)aw**) means "please," ຂອຍ (**k(h)awy**) means "I," and ຄວາຍ (**kuuay**: the long **uua** sounds like **waa**) means "water buffalo."

52.1

ຂອງ **k(h)awng**
ຂອງຂອຍບໍ? **k(h)awng k(ha)wy baw?**
ຂອງຂອຍ. **k(h)awng k(h)awy.**
ຂໍ **k(h)aw**
ຂອຍ **k(h)awy**
ຄວາຍ **kuuay**

ດຽວ (**diao**) is a classifier that is generally placed after a noun to mean only one of that noun. For example, ຄົນດຽວ (**kon diao**) means "only me; just one person," "alone," or "just me" (if you're talking about yourself).

2.2 ດຽວ **diao**

Do not use ຕົວະ (**dtua**) in any accusing manner. Lao people don't raise their voices often, but this could cause a flareup of emotions, just as it would anywhere else.

Exercises

A. Translate into English:

1. ຂ້ອຍຮູ້ຜົວຂອງດາວ
2. ກິນລາວ
3. ບ້ອຍຮຽນຫຍາຍໆ
4. ຮອນຫຍາຍ

5. ບ້ອຍຂອກທາຍໆສູບ
6. ມີບໍ່?
7. ບໍ່ມີ
8. ຂ້ອຍມີວຽກຫຍາຍ

Now listen to these words/phrases, pronounced on the CD. Repeat each one several times to practice.

B: Translate into Lao:

1. Only one person.
2. I don't smoke.
3. Stop!
4. You still don't know?
5. My friend's husband ate my water buffalo.
6. Ask Nawy, "Do you know Nok?"
7. He lies a lot.
8. The mosquito is smaller than the white bird.
9. Do you eat shrimp?
10. Women write better than men.

Now listen to these words/phrases, pronounced on the CD. Repeat each one several times to practice.

LESSON 14

Left Side Only Vowels

LAO LETTER	ALPHABETICAL ORDER	ENGLISH SOUND	ENGLISH LETTER
ເx	12	as in game (long)	*eei*
ແx	15	as in air (long)	*aae*

Example of ເx sound: ເອລາ
Examples of ແx sound: ແດ່, ແລ້ວ

LAO LETTER	ALPHABETICAL ORDER	ENGLISH SOUND	ENGLISH LETTER
ໂx	18	as in phone (long)	*oo*
ໃx, ໄx	35, 36	as in hi (short & long)	*ai*

Examples of ໂx sound: ໂພດ, ໂດລາ
Example of ໃx / ໄx sound: ໃຈ / ໄປ

Exercises

A. Write in English:

1. ເອລາ
2. ແຂບ
3. ໃຈ
4. ບອນ
5. ລິມ
6. ແຂງແຮງ
7. ໄປ

8. ໄກ
9. ແດງ
10. ໂຈນ
11. ມີ
12. ໂອ
13. ຄິກັນ
14. ໂດລາ

15. ແລ້ວ
16. ໂພດ
17. ຍຸງ
18. ແຕ່ງງານ
19. ທາຍ
20. ແພງ

Now listen to these words/phrases, pronounced on the CD.
Repeat each one several times to practice.

B. Write in Lao:

1.	yaa nawy	11.	poot
2.	joon	12.	wai
3.	tai	13.	gung
4.	soodaa	14.	dtaaeng ngaan
5.	kon laao	15.	jai
6.	weei laa	16.	doo laa
7.	dtaaek	17.	hoong maw
8.	moong	18.	yaak maa
9.	tam ma daa	19.	nai look
10.	saaep	20.	maak dtaaeng

Now listen to these words/phrases, pronounced on the CD.
Repeat each one several times to practice.

C. Put the following words in alphabetical order:

1. ໄວ, ໄຂກດິ, ຜູ້ສາວ, ໃຈ, ໄກ
2. ໂພດ, ຢາ, ຕົວະ, ຜົວ, ແຂບ, ໝາກແຕງ, ໂຮງໝໍ
3. ເວລາ, ກັບ, ແຕງ, ແລ້ວ, ໃບ, ແພງ, ຈີ້, ດິ, ໄທ

LESSON 15
Vocabulary D

#	LAO	ENGLISH	TRANSLATION(S)
1	ໄກ	gai	far (*adj*)
2	ແຂງແຮງ	khaaeng haaeng	healthy (*adj*)
3	ໂຈນ	joon	criminal (*n*)
4	ໃຈ	jai	heart (*n*)
5	ໃສ່	sai	with, use; put on/in (*v*)
6	ແຊບ	saaep	delicious (*adj*)
7	ໂຊກດີ	sook dii	good luck, goodbye
8	ສີແດງ	sii daaeng	red (*adj*)
9	ແດ່	daae	please
10	ໂດລາ	doo laa	U.S. $ dollar (*n*)
11	ໄດ້	dai	can, able; received; did (*v*)
12	ແຕກ	dtaaek	break (*v*)
13	ແຕ່ງງານ	dtaaeng ngaan	marry (*v*)
14	ປະເທດໄທ	pba teeit tai	Thailand (*n*)
15	ໄປ	pbai	go (*v*)
16	ໃນ	nai	in
17	ແຟນ	faaen	girlfriend/boyfriend (*n*)
18	ແພງ	paaeng	expensive (*adj*)
19	ໂພດ	poot	too much (*adv*)

20	ໄຟ	**fai**	fire (*n*)
21	ໝາກແຕງ	**maak dtaaeng**	cucumber (*n*)
22	ໂມງ	**moong**	o'clock, clock, watch (*n*)
23	ແລ້ວ	**laaeo**	already (*adv*); finish(ed)
24	ເວລາ	**weei laa**	time (*n*)
25	ໄວ	**wai**	fast (*adj*)
26	ໂຮງຮຽນ	**hoong hian**	school (*n*)
27	ໃຫ້	**hai**	give (*v*)

ໂຊກດີ (**sook dii**) is used primarily to say "goodbye" by the person who is stay-ing behind. The person leaving usually says ລາກ່ອນ (**laa gawn**). ໂຊກດີ also means "Good luck."

ສີ (**sii**) means "color." ແດງ (**daaeng**) means "red." Always use ສີ before a color, as in ສີແດງ ("color red").

ແດ່ (**daae**) is a common word that means "please." It is usually placed after the request, and is sometimes used in conjunction with ຂໍ but that is not necessary. **k(h)aw sawng jawk daae** means "Please bring two cups."

ໄດ້ (**dai**) means "can," as in ability. To ask for a discount, you would ask: **lut dai baw?** The answer will be: **dai** (can) or **baw dai** (can't).

ໂພດ (**poot**) means "too," but is used *after* adjectives. For example, **paaeng poot** means "Too expensive."

ໂມງ (**moong**) is used to talk about the time of day. For example, **jak moong** means "What time (will something happen)?" The answer will be a time, such as 1:00 P.M. ເວລາ (**weei laa**) refers to "time" in the general sense, such as: ບໍ່ມີເວລາ (**baw mii weei laa**), which is a common expression that means: "I don't have time."

ແລ້ວ (**laaeo**) is one of the most common words in Lao. It is usually used to signify that something has finished, and is often translated as "already." For example, **gin laaeo baw**? means, "Have you (already) eaten?" **gin laaeo** means, "I've already eaten."

ໃຫ້ (**hai**) is used alone to mean "give," and it also used in conjunction with ເອົາ (**ow**) "take"—to mean "give something to someone." For example, **ow bik hai khawy** means, "Take (the) pen (to) give me," or "Give me (a/the) pen."

60

ໂຊກດີ **sook dii.**
ລາກ່ອນ **laa gawn.**

ສີ **sii**
ສີແດງ **sii daaeng** ("color red")

ແດ່ **daae**
ຂໍສອງຈອກແດ່ **k(h)aw sawng jawk daae.** (Please bring two cups.)

ໄດ້ **dai**
ຫຼຸດໄດ້ບໍ່? **lut dai baw?** (Can I have a discount?)
ໄດ້ **dai.** (You can have a discount.)
ບໍ່ໄດ້ **baw dai.** (You can't have a discount.)

ໂພດ **poot**
ແພງໂພດ **paaeng poot.** (Too expensive.)

ໂມງ **moong**
ບໍ່ມີເວລາ **baw mii weei laa.** (I don't have time.)

ແລ້ວ **laaeo**
ກິນແລ້ວບໍ່? **gin laaeo baw?** (Have you eaten yet?)
ກິນແລ້ວ **gin laaeo.** (I've already eaten.)

ໃຫ້ **hai**
ເອົາ **ow**
ເອົາບິກໃຫ້ຂ້ອຍ **ow bik hai khawy.** (Give me a/the pen.)

Exercises

A. Translate into English:

1. ແຊບບໍ່?
2. ບ່ອຍແຕ່ງງານແລ້ວ
3. ລາວຍັງບໍ່ມີແຟນ
4. ຈັກໂມງແລ້ວ?

5. ໄປໄວໆໄດ້ບໍ່?
6. ບໍ່ມີເວລາ
7. ໄປໂຮງຮຽນຈັກໂມງ?
8. ຫມາກແຕງແພງຫລາຍໂພດ

Now listen to these words/phrases, pronounced on the CD.
Repeat each one several times to practice.

B. Translate into Lao:

1. Good luck!
2. What time does the market close?
3. I will go to work at 10 o'clock.
4. Lao (language) is not too difficult.
5. My glass is (already) broken.
6. I already ate.
7. The strong man wants to marry the pretty woman.
8. Can you write Lao?

Note: The number "10" is written ສິບ (**sip**).

Now listen to these words/phrases, pronounced on the CD.
Repeat each one several times to practice.

LESSON 16

Left & Top Vowels

LAO LETTER	ALPHABETICAL ORDER	ENGLISH SOUND	ENGLISH LETTER
ເⅩ̌	11	as in b*et* (short)	*e*

Examples of ເⅩ̌ sound: ເດັກ, ເຍັບ, ເຈັບ

LAO	ALPHABETICAL ORDER	ENGLISH SOUND	ENGLISH LETTER
ເⅩ̂	23	as in numbe(*r*) (short)	(*er*)
ເⅩ̂	24	as in numbe(*r*) (long)	(*err*)

Examples of ເⅩ̂ sound: ເຄີ່ງ, ເງິນ, ເບິ່ງ

Example of ເⅩ̂ sound alone: ເຜີ

Examples of ເⅩ̂ sound followed by a consonant: ເປີດ, ເຂີນ

The (*er*) and (*err*) transliterations are widely used, but are not entirely accurate. They do come close to the sound required, but with this caveat: the "*r*" sound is more pronounced when nothing follows the "*r*," and only slightly spoken, if at all, when a consonant follows.

Exercises

A. Translate into English:

1.	ເປິດ	8.	ຄິກັນ	15.	ເງິນ
2.	ເຢັນ	9.	ເຈັບ	16.	ເຮັດ
3.	ເຂີນ	10.	ເບິ່ງ	17.	ເປັນ
4.	ໃຫ້	11.	ເຄີຍ	18.	ເໜັນ
5.	ເດັກ	12.	ເຜັດ	19.	ເຄິ່ງ
6.	ເຜີ	13.	ເຄັນ	20.	ເຕັນ
7.	ເວລາ	14.	ແລວ		

Now listen to these words/phrases, pronounced on the CD.
Repeat each one several times to practice.

B. Write in Lao:

1.	ng(er)n	8.	k(h)aw	15.	phet
2.	kem	9.	het	16.	saaep
3.	men	10.	k(err)'y	17.	k(er)ng
4.	f(err)	11.	paaeng poot	18.	ngaam laai
5.	s(err)n	12.	dek	19.	b(er)ng
6.	nok nawy	13.	yen	20.	nai
7.	jep	14.	pben		

Now listen to these words/phrases, pronounced on the CD.
Repeat each one several times to practice.

C. Put the following words in alphabetical order:

1. ເປັນ, ໃຫ້, ເຄັນ, ເວລາ, ເຕັນ, ເດັກ
2. ເຜີ, ເປິດ, ເຜັດ, ເງິນ, ເຄິ່ງ, ຄິກັນ, ເຄີຍ
3. ເຮັດ, ເຈັບ, ເບິ່ງ, ເດັກ, ເຄັນ, ເປັນ, ເງິນ, ເຂີນ

LESSON 17
Vocabulary E

#	LAO	ENGLISH	TRANSLATION(S)
1	ເຄັມ	kem	salty (adj)
2	ເຄິ່ງ	k(er)ng	½ (one half)
3	ເຄີຍ	k(err)'y	have ever
4	ເງິນ	ng(er)n	money (n)
5	ເຈັບ	jep	hurt (v), (adj)
6	ເຊີນ	s(err)n	invite (v)
7	ເດັກນ້ອຍ	dek nawy	child (n)
8	ເຕັມ	dtem	full (for cups, etc.) (adj)
9	ເປັນ	bpen	am, is (for people)
10	ເປິດ	bp(er)t	open (v)
11	ເຜັດ	p(h)et	spicy (adj)
12	ເຝີ	f(err)	rice noodle dish (n)
13	ເຢັນ	yen	cool (adj)
14	ເໝັນ	men	stinks (adj)
15	ເຮັດ	het	do (v)

ເຄິ່ງ (k(er)ng) means "half" and is often used when telling the time. For example, **sawng moong k(er)ng** means "2:30."

ເຄີຍ (k(err)y) means "have ever" and "have never," depending on its placement in the sentence. For example, **jow k(err)y bpai bpateeit thai baw?**

translates to "<u>Have you ever</u> been to Luang Prabang?" And **<u>baw k(err)y</u> (pbai)** means "I haven't (ever) been" or "I've never been."

ເປັນ **(pben)** is used to say that a person "is" something. For example, **khawy bpen aajaan sawn** means "I am a teacher."

ເຮັດ **(het)** means "do/make," and needs to be followed by an object, verb or question word. For example, **jow <u>het wiak</u> laai baw?** means "Do you work a lot?" and **jow <u>het nyang</u>?** means "What are you doing?"

ເຖິງ **k(er)ng**
ສອງໂມງເຖິງ **sawng moong k(er)ng** (2:30)

ເຄີຍ **k(err)y**
ເຈົ້າເຄີຍໄປປະເທດໄທບໍ່? **jow k(err)y bpai bpateeit thai baw?** (Have you ever been to Luang Prabang?)
ບໍ່ເຄີຍ(ໄປ). **baw k(err)y (pbai).** (I haven't [ever] been. *or* I've never been.)

ເປັນ **pben**
ຂ້ອຍເປັນອາຈານສອນ. **khawy bpen aajaan sawn.** (I am a teacher.)

ເຮັດ **het**
ເຈົ້າເຮັດວຽກຫຼາຍບໍ່? **jow het wiak laai baw?** (Do you work a lot?)
ເຈົ້າເຮັດຫຍັງ? **jow het nyang?** (What are you doing?)

ສາມ **(saam)** is the number "3." To say "30," for example, you would say "3" (**saam**) and then "10" (**sip**). Hence: **saam sip** means "30." To say the number "13," you would reverse this: "10" **sip** and then "3" **saam** would be **sip saam**, or "13."

ສາມ **saam** (3)
ສິບສາມ **sip saam** (13)
ສາມສິບ **saam sip** (30)

ຫຍັງ? **(nyang)** means "what?" when combined with a verb. For example, **het nyang** (What are you doing?) literally means, "Do what?" In common speech, the subject "you" is understood. **maaen nyang** literally means "Is what?" but in everyday speech it just means "What?" as in "What? (I didn't quite hear you)."

ຫຍັງ **nyang**

68.2 ເຮັດຫຍັງ? **het nyang?** (What are you doing?)

ແມ່ນຫຍັງ? **maaen nyang?** (What? [I didn't quite hear you.])

Exercises

A. Translate into English:

1. ມີຊາເຢັນບໍ່?
2. ເຄີຍໄປປະເທດໄທບໍ່?
3. ເຈັບ!
4. ສອງໂມງເຄິ່ງ

5. ຂ້ອຍບໍ່ມີເງິນຫຼາຍ
6. ເຜັດຫຼາຍບໍ່?
7. ເດັກນ້ອຍເຮັດຫຍັງ?
8. ມີເວລາບໍ່?

69 Now listen to these words/phrases, pronounced on the CD. Repeat each one several times to practice.

B. Translate into Lao:

1. The *f(err)* is really spicy.
2. Look at him.
3. The fish is too salty.
4. Have you already been?
5. I haven't been yet.
6. Can you come to my house at 3:30?
7. She is a man.
8. Is it delicious?

70 Now listen to these words/phrases, pronounced on the CD. Repeat each one several times to practice.

LESSON 18

Left & Right Vowels

LAO LETTER	ALPHABETICAL ORDER	ENGLISH SOUND	ENGLISH LETTER
ເXະ	10	as in net (short & rarely written)	e
ແXະ ແໍXX (rare)	13, 14	as in air or eh (short)	ae

Examples of ເXະ sound: ເຊະ, ເມຍ
Example of ແXະ / ແໍXX sound: ແລະ, ແບະບຳ

LAO LETTER	ALPHABETICAL ORDER	ENGLISH SOUND	ENGLISH LETTER
ໂXະ	16	as in go or oh (short)	o
ເXາະ	19	mix aw & o as in naughty (very short)	aw
ເXຍ ເໍXJ (rare spelling)	26	as in U.S. via or U.K. ear (long)	iaa

Examples of ໂXະ sound: ໂຕະ, ໂຊະ
Examples of ເXາະ sound: ເບາະ, ເພາະວ່າ
Examples of ເXຍ sound: ເບຍ, ເມຍ

Exercises

A. Write in English:

1. ແລະ
2. ເຊະ
3. ແຜັດ

4. ເມຍ
5. ເພາະວ່າ
6. ເບາະ

7. ເງິນ
8. ຍາກ
9. ໂຕະ

10. ແນະນຳ	13. ເສຍ	16. ຍຸງ
11. ເຕະ	14. ໂຊະ	17. ເຊີນ
12. ຈອກ	15. ເບຍ	

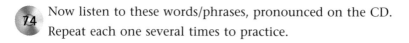

Now listen to these words/phrases, pronounced on the CD.
Repeat each one several times to practice.

B. Write in Lao:

1. lae	6. dto	11. s(err)n
2. saw	7. nyung	12. naw
3. dte	8. paw waa	13. jawk
4. nae nam	9. ng(er)n	14. yaak
5. miaa	10. siaa	15. so

Now listen to these words/phrases, pronounced on the CD.
Repeat each one several times to practice.

C. Put in alphabetical order:

1. ເຕະ, ຍາກ, ເພາະວ່າ, ໂຕະ
2. ແລະ, ເນາະ, ແນະນຳ, ເຜັດ, ໂຊະ
3. ເຊະ, ເສຍ, ຍຸງ, ແນະນຳ, ຍາກ, ກິນ

LESSON 19

Vocabulary F

#	LAO	ENGLISH	TRANSLATION(S)
1	ເສຍ	siaa	lose something (*v*)
2	ເຊະ	se	*get the heck out of here!* (for dogs)
3	ໂຊະ	so	*get out of here!* (for chickens)
4	ເຕະ	dte	kick (*v*)
5	ໂຕະ	dto	desk, table (*n*)
6	ແນະນຳ	nae nam	introduce (*v*); advice
7	ເນາະ	naw	huh? right?
8	ເບຍ	biaa	beer (n)
9	ເພາະວ່າ	paw waa	because
10	ເມຍ	miaa	wife (*n*)
11	ແລະ	lae	and (for nouns)

The written structure ເxJ is almost obsolete; ເxຍ has taken its place. You will see this on T-shirts and beer bottles that read: ເບຍລາວ (**biaa laao**). "Beer Lao" is the country's only domestically produced beer label.

Exercises

A. Translate into English:

1. ແບະນຳໝູ່ຂອງຂ້ອຍ
2. ກິນປາເພາະວ່າແຊບຫຼາຍ
3. ດາວແລະນ້ອຍເຄີຍໄປລາວ
4. ແພງຫຼາຍເນາະ
5. ໄຂະ!
6. ເມຍນ້ອຍຂອງລາວສູບຢາຫຼາຍ
7. ລາວກິນຫຍັງ?
8. ນິກເສຍຄວາຍຂອງເມຍລາວ

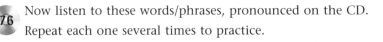

Now listen to these words/phrases, pronounced on the CD.
Repeat each one several times to practice.

B. Translate into Lao:

1. It's really hard (difficult), huh?
2. Has she ever eaten *f(err)*?
3. I don't have money because I eat a lot.
4. It's hot, huh?
5. Do you like my desk?
6. This is too spicy, huh.
7. My friend's husband lost my water buffalo.

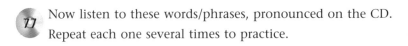

Now listen to these words/phrases, pronounced on the CD.
Repeat each one several times to practice.

LESSON 20
Left, Top & Right Vowels

LAO LETTER	ALPHABETICAL ORDER	ENGLISH SOUND	ENGLISH LETTER
ເxືອ (rare)	29	as in *look* + *ah* (short)	*uh'a*
ເxືອ	30	as in *look* + *ah* (long)	*uhh'a*

Examples of ເxືອ sound: ເຮືອ, ເມືອຍ

LAO LETTER	ALPHABETICAL ORDER	ENGLISH SOUND	ENGLISH LETTER
ເxົາ	34	as in n*ow*	*ow*

Examples of ເxົາ sound: ເອົາ, ເຈົ້າ, ເຖົ້າ, ເບົາ

The vowel ເxົາ is often transcribed as **ao**, but we use **ow** as it better corresponds to English words such *as now, how, cow, wow* and *vow*. Do not get confused when you see **bow** and **tow**, though—they too are pronounced with the **ow** as in *now*.

Exercises

A. Write in English:

1. ເຈົ້າ
2. ເຮືອ
3. ຮຽນ
4. ເມືອຍ
5. ເຮືອນ
6. ເຖົ້າ
7. ເຫື້ອຫນຳ

8. ເຄື່ອງ
9. ປິດ
10. ເມົາ
11. ແລະ
12. ແຕ່ງງານ
13. ເດືອນ
14. ເອົາ

15. ເລືອດ
16. ເມືອງ
17. ເບົາ
18. ເວົ້າ
19. ເມືອກ
20. ເຮັດ

Now listen to these words/phrases, pronounced on the CD.
Repeat each one several times to practice.

B. Write in Lao:

1. duhh'an	8. ow	15. mow
2. wow	9. naw	16. muhh'ay
3. huhh'an	10. luhh'at	17. muhh'ak
4. k(h)aao	11. huhh'a	18. muhh'ang
5. het	12. kuhh'ang	19. bow
6. jow	13. daao	20. tuhh'a naa
7. t(h)ow	14. saaep	

 Now listen to these words/phrases, pronounced on the CD.
Repeat each one several times to practice.

C. Arrange in alphabetical order:

1. ເມືອງ, ເຈົ້າ, ເລືອດ, ປິດ, ເບິ່ງ
2. ແລະ, ເຫື່ອຫນ້າ, ເມື້ອຍ, ເອົາ, ເກົ້າ, ເອົ້າ, ເມືອກ
3. ເມົ້າ, ເດືອນ, ເຮັດ, ເຮືອ, ເຫື່ອຫນ້າ, ເບົາ, ເລືອດ, ເຄື່ອງ

LESSON 21

Vocabulary G

#	LAO	ENGLISH	TRANSLATION(S)
1	ພວກເຂົາ	puak k(h)ow	they, them
2	ເຄື່ອງ	kuhh'ang	thing (*n*)
3	ເຈົ້າ	jow	you
4	ເສື້ອ	suhh'a	shirt (*n*)
5	ເດືອນ	duhh'an	month, moon (*n*)
6	ເດົາ	dow	guess (*n*), (*v*)
7	ເຖົ້າ	t(h)ow	old (*adj*)
8	ເບົາ	bow	light, soft (not heavy) (*adj*)
9	ເມືອງ	muhh'ang	city (*n*)
10	ເມືອກ	muhh'ak	humid; oily (*adj*)
11	ເມື່ອຍ	muhh'ay	tired (*adj*)
12	ເມົາ	mow	drunk (*adj*)
13	ເລືອດ	luhh'at	blood (*n*)
14	ເວົ້າ	wow	say, speak (*v*)
15	ເອົາ	ow	take (*v*)
16	ເຮືອ	huhh'a	boat (*n*)
17	ເຮືອດ	huhh'at	bed bugs (*n*)
18	ເຮືອນ	huhh'an	house (*n*)

ພວກເຂົາ (**puak k(h)ow**) is the proper way to say "they" or "them." Do not confuse it with **puak how** ("we").

ເບົາ (**bow**) can be combined with other words to create new ones. This is very common practice in Lao. For example, **huu bow** (ຫູເບົາ) literally translates as "ear soft" *(soft ear)* or "gullible."

ເລືອດ (**luhh'at**) is put in many Lao dishes. If you don't want it, you'll be better off learning how to say **baw sai luhh'at,** which literally means "not with blood," or simply "without blood."

ເອົາ (**ow**) is used to ask for something or ask if someone wants something. For example, "**ow baw?**" ເອົາບໍ່? means "Do you want it?" ເອົາ (**ow**) means "I'll take it."

ເອົາ can also be combined with other words: **ow maa** (ເອົາມາ) literally means "take come," that is, "bring," and **ow pbai** (ເອົາໄປ) literally means "take go": simply, "take."

83 ພວກເຂົາ **puak k(h)ow**

ເບົາ **bow**
ຫູເບົາ **huu bow** (gullible)

ເລືອດ **luhh'at**
ບໍ່ໃສ່ເລືອດ **baw sai luhh'at.** (Not with blood. [regarding food])

ເອົາ **ow**
ເອົາບໍ່? **ow baw?** (Do you want it?)
ເອົາ **ow.** (I'll take it.)
ບໍ່ເອົາ **baw ow.** (I don't want it.)

ເອົາມາ **ow maa** (bring)
ເອົາໄປ **ow pbai** (take)

Exercises

A. Translate into English:

1. ເຈົ້າມີແຟນແລ້ວບໍ?
2. ພວກເຮົາເມົາແລ້ວ
3. ລາວເວົ້າຫຍັງ?
4. ເຮົາໃຫ້ຂ້ອຍແດ່
5. ເມືອງຫຼາຍແບບະ?
6. ເຈົ້າຢາກໄປເດືອນໜ້າບໍ?
7. ເມົ່ອຍບໍ?
8. ຄົນລາວມັກເວົ້າວ່າບໍເປັນຫຍັງ

Now listen to these words/phrases, pronounced on the CD. Repeat each one several times to practice.

Notes:
ໜ້າ (**naa**) means "face," "in front" and "next."

ບໍເປັນຫຍັງ (**baw pben nyang**) is one of the most common phrases in Lao. It means "Never mind" or "Don't worry about it."

B. Translate into Lao:

1. Did you already tell him?
2. I'll take F(err) without blood.
3. Do you remember me?
4. You're very pretty, too.
5. Two cups, please.
6. Water buffaloes are better than bed bugs.
7. What did you lose?
8. Are you drunk (already)?

Now listen to these words/phrases, pronounced on the CD. Repeat each one several times to practice.

86 Vowels in Alphabetical Order as Found in Dictionary:

1. xะ	14. แไx้x	27. xฺx
2. x̆x	15. แxx	28. เxอ
3. xๅ	16. ไขะ	29. เx̂อ
4. x̂	17. x̂x	30. x̂อะ
5. x̆	18. ไx	31. x̆อะ
6. x̆	19. เxๅะ	32. x̂อ
7. x̂	20. x̊	33. xอx
8. xฺ	21. xอx	34. ใx
9. xฺ	22. เx̂	35. ไx
10. เxะ	23. เx̂	36. เx̂ๅ
11. เx̆x	24. เxฺ̆ะ	37. xๅ
12. เx	25. xฺ̆x	38. xอย
13. แxะ	26. เxย, (เxฺ̆)	

REVIEW 3
LESSON 23

Here are some of the most useful words and phrases you have learned.

Exercises

A. Give the English meanings:

1. ໄປ	11. ຍຸງ	21. ແລ້ວ
2. ເຄີຍ	12. ເບິ່ງ	22. ຜິວ
3. ບໍ່	13. ຕະຫຼາດ	23. ກິນ
4. ຜູ້ຊາຍ	14. ແຟນ	24. ແຕ່ງງານ
5. ເມາະ	15. ຮຽນ	25. ອັງກິດ
6. ລາວ	16. ເພ້	26. ເຜັດ
7. ເອົາ	17. ຢາສູບ	27. ລືມ
8. ໂຊກດີ	18. ຄິນດຽວ	28. ມາ
9. ທຳມະດາ	19. ເຮັດວຽກ	29. ເຈົ້າ
10. ຂອງຂອຍ	20. ບິດ	30. ນ້ອຍ

Now listen to these words/phrases, pronounced on the CD.
Repeat each one several times to practice.

B. Write the Lao:

1. have	11. very pretty	21. friend
2. hot	12. delicious	22. speak
3. fish	13. can	23. water
4. tell	14. not	24. know
5. return home	15. money	25. lose, pay
6. woman yet	16. want	26. like
7. remember	17. sleep	27. too expensive
8. 10:30	18. stop	28. fast
9. tired	19. better	29. time
10. wife	20. open	30. heart

Now listen to these words/phrases, pronounced on the CD.
Repeat each one several times to practice.

C. Put in alphabetical order:

1. ຮຽນ, ຍັງ, ຕະຫຼາດ, ລາວ, ແຊບ, ບໍ່
2. ຍາກ, ເນາະ, ດາວ, ພູ່, ຄິກັນ, ປາ, ເວົ້າ, ເສຍ, ບອກ
3. ເມົາ, ກັບ, ຜູ້ສາວ, ຫຼາຍ, ໃຈ, ປິດ, ແດງ, ຂ້ອຍ, ເຈັ້າ, ນ້ຳ, ເຜິ

D. Translate into Lao:

   1.   Have you already eaten?
   2.   I'm very tired.
   3.   What time is it?
   4.   Are you (already) married?
   5.   Very delicious.
   6.   It's hot, huh?
   7.   Have you ever been to Thailand?
   8.   Can you go faster?
   9.   I don't have time.
 10. I want to eat spicy *F(err)*.
 11. Tell him what you told me.
 12. I don't speak Lao very well yet.
 13. Do you smoke?
 14. I will go to sleep. (I'm going to sleep.)
 15. Don't you remember me?

Note:
ພາສາ (**paasaa**) means "language" and is stated before the language referred
to. For example, **paasaa laao** (ພາສາລາວ).

Now listen to these words/phrases, pronounced on the CD.
Repeat each one several times to practice.

E. Translate into English:

1. ຂ້ອຍຈະກັບບ້ານສອງໂມງເຄິ່ງ
2. ເຈົ້າໃຈດີ
3. ຮ້ອນເນາະ?
4. ໝູ່ຂອງຂ້ອຍມັກນອນຫວາຍໆ
5. ແພງໂພດເນາະ
6. ພໍ່ເຈົ້າເຮັດວຽກຫຍັງ?
7. ເມົາແລ້ວບໍ່?
8. ແຊບບໍ່?
9. ລາວເວົ້າພາສາລາວດີກ່ວາຂ້ອຍ
10. ຖາມລາວແດ່
11. ເອົາເງິນມາ
12. ລາວມີແຟນແລ້ວບໍ່?
13. ຂ້ອຍບໍ່ເຄີຍກິນຢຸງ
14. ເມຍຂອງໝູ່ຂ້ອຍຮູ້ພໍ່ຂອງໝູ່ມິກ
15. ກິນແລ້ວບໍ່?

Now listen to these words/phrases, pronounced on the CD.
Repeat each one several times to practice.

LESSON 24
Extra Vocabulary

In alphabetical order:

#	LAO	ENGLISH	TRANSLATION(S)
1	ຂອບໃຈ	k(h)awp jai	thank you
2	ເຂົ້າໃຈ	k(h)ow jai	understand (*v*)
3	ຂົວມິດຕະພາບ	k(h)uua mit dtaapaap	The Friendship Bridge (*n*)
4	ສະບາຍດີ	sabaaidii	hello, good
5	ໂທລະສັບ	toolasaap	phone (*n*), call (*v*)
6	ເທົ່າໃດ?	tow dai	how much?
7	ແນວໃດ?	naaeo dai	how?
8	ເປັນຫຍັງ?	pben nyang	why?
9	ພົບ, ເຈິ	pop, j(er)	meet (*v*)
10	ແມ່ນບໍ່?	maaen baw	really?, right?
11	(ແມ່ນ)ໃຜ?	(maaen) p(h)ai	who?
12	(ແມ່ນ)ຫຍັງ?	(maaen) nyang	what?
13	ເມື່ອໃດ?	muhh'a dai	when?
14	(ຢູ່)ໃສ?	(yuu) sai	where?
15	ໜາວ	naao	cold (*adj*)
16	ຫຼຸດໄດ້ບໍ່?	lut dai baw?	Can I have a discount?
17	ອີ່ມ	iim	full (not hungry)

ສະບາຍດີບໍ? (**sabaaidii baww**) means "How are you?"
ສະບາຍດີ is the most common answer, which means "Good, fine." When used alone as a statement, it means "Hello."

Person A: ສະບາຍດີ (Hello.)
Person B: ສະບາຍດີ (Hi.)

Person A: ສະບາຍດີບໍ? (How are you?)
Person B: ສະບາຍດີ (Good.)

The letter ໆ is unspoken, but signals to the reader that the word before it is to be repeated. For example, **k(h)awp jai lai lai** means "Thank you very, very much."

ຂອບໃຈຫຼາຍໆ **k(h)awp jai lai lai** (Thank you very, very much.)

Answer Key

Answer Key

Lessons 1–7

Lesson 1

A.

1. daw
2. jaw
3. gaw
4. dtaw
5. jaw
6. daw
7. gaw
8. jaw
9. dtaw
10. gaw

B.

1. ด
2. ง
3. ต
4. จ
5. ต
6. ง
7. จ
8. ต
9. ด
10. ง

Lesson 2

A.

1. daw
2. jaw
3. dtaw
4. yaw
5. aw
6. bpaw
7. baw
8. aw
9. dtaw
10. bpaw
11. jaw
12. aw
13. baw
14. yaw
15. gaw
16. daw

B.

1. อ
2. ย
3. ป
4. ต
5. ง
6. อ
7. จ
8. บ
9. ง
10. ด
11. อ
12. จ
13. ป
14. ด
15. ย
16. อ

Lesson 3

A.

1. daw	9. saw	17. kaw
2. saw	10. dtaw	18. yaw
3. gaw	11. jaw	19. baw
4. ngaw	12. daw	20. dtaw
5. bpaw	13. naw	21. gaw
6. jaw	14. ngaw	22. aw
7. nyaw	15. baw	23. naw
8. kaw	16. bpaw	24. saw

B.

1. ຕ	9. ຍ	17. ຊ
2. ດ	10. ປ	18. ກ
3. ງ	11. ຫ	19. ບ
4. ຊ	12. ອ	20. ປ
5. ນ	13. ຍ	21. ງ
6. ບ	14. ດ	22. ບ
7. ຕ	15. ຈ	23. ຕ
8. ງ	16. ຕ	24. ດ

Lesson 4

A.

1. paw	11. kaw	21. daw
2. maw	12. jaw	22. law
3. taw	13. dtaw	23. yaw
4. daw	14. saw	24. haw
5. faw	15. naw	25. maw
6. waw	16. nyaw	26. paw
7. law	17. taw	27. taw
8. baw	18. waw	28. aw
9. haw	19. ngaw	29. bpaw
10. paw	20. gaw	30. daw

B.

1. ດ	11. ບ	21. ຕ
2. ພ	12. ຕ	22. ຄ
3. ລ	13. ມ	23. ນ
4. ມ	14. ວ	24. ປ
5. ນ	15. ພ	25. ວ
6. ອ	16. ຍ	26. ງ
7. ຊ	17. ຍ	27. ຍ
8. ຈ	18. ຊ	28. ກ
9. ຜ	19. ງ	29. ຍ
10. ພ	20. ທ	30. ຜ

Lesson 5

A.

1. paw	11. law	21. naw	31. yaw
2. naw	12. baw	22. nyaw	32. k(h)aw
3. k(h)aw	13. haw	23. taw	33. haw
4. maw	14. p(h)aw	24. t(h)aw	34. maw
5. taw	15. haw	25. waw	35. faw
6. daw	16. paw	26. ngaw	36. p(h)aw
7. faw	17. kaw	27. haw	37. taw
8. waw	18. jaw	28. gaw	38. aw
9. saw	19. dtaw	29. daw	39. bpaw
10. haw	20. saw	30. law	40. haw

B.

1. ດ	11. ບ	21. ຕ	31. ທ, ຣ
2. ພ	12. ຄ	22. ຂ	32. ຈ
3. ລ	13. ມ	23. ນ	33. ມ
4. ມ	14. ວ	24. ປ	34. ຜ
5. ນ	15. ຝ, ຟ	25. ວ	35. ພ
6. ອ	16. ຍ	26. ງ	36. ລ
7. ທ, ຣ	17. ຍ	27. ຍ	37. ຝ, ຟ
8. ຈ	18. ສ, ຊ	28. ກ	38. ຕ
9. ຖ	19. ງ	29. ຍ	39. ສ, ຊ
10. ຜ	20. ທ	30. ຟ, ຝ	40. ນ

Lesson 6
A.

1. haw	19. waw	37. gaw
2. taw	20. law	38. haw
3. saw	21. bpaw	39. law
4. saw	22. p(h)aw	40. baw
5. faw	23. baw	41. nyaw
6. nyaw	24. law	42. naw
7. gaw	25. waw	43. haw
8. paw	26. faw	44. paw
9. naw	27. ngaw	45. yaw
10. nyaw	28. maw	46. faw
11. law	29. aw	47. t(h)aw
12. maw	30. haw	48. kaw
13. jaw	31. p(h)aw	49. dtaw
14. naw	32. ngaw	50. nyaw
15. t(h)aw	33. maw	51. saw
16. k(h)aw	34. law	52. naw
17. dtaw	35. saw	
18. kaw	36. daw	

B.

1. ກ	15. ຂ	29. ປ
2. ຂ	16. ບ	30. ຢ
3. ວ, ຫວ	17. ມ, ໝ	31. ກ
4. ພ	18. ນ, ໜ	32. ຄ
5. ທ	19. ປ	33. ນ, ໜ
6. ສ, ຊ	20. ຜ, ພ	34. ຈ
7. ຢ	21. ຖ	35. ທ
8. ທ, ຮ	22. ຍ, ຫຍ	36. ວ, ຫວ
9. ລ, ຫຼ, ຫລ	23. ງ, ຫງ	37. ທ, ຮ
10. ຈ	24. ໜ	38. ຍ, ຫຍ
11. ຕ	25. ລ, ຫຼ, ຫລ	39. ພ
12. ຜ, ຜ	26. ສ, ຊ	40. ຢ
13. ອ	27. ທ	41. ມ, ໝ
14. ກ	28. ຕ	42. ກ

43. ອ	47. ຜ	51. ດ
44. ຖ	48. ລ, ຫຼ, ຫລ	52. ມ, ໝ
45. ພ, ຜ	49. ບ	
46. ງ, ຫງ	50. ປ	

Lesson 7

1. gaw	12. taw	23. waw
2. k(h)aw	13. naw	24. haw
3. kaw	14. baw	25. ngaw
4. ngaw	15. bpaw	26. nyaw
5. jaw	16. p(h)aw	27. naw
6. saw	17. faw	28. maw
7. saw	18. paw	29. law
8. nyaw	19. faw	30. waw
9. daw	20. maw	31. aw
10. dtaw	21. yaw	32. haw
11. t(h)aw	22. law	

Lessons 8–18

Lesson 8

A.

1. ja	8. bpaa	15. t(h)aam
2. maa	9. laao	16. tamlaai
3. naam	10. ngaam	17. haak
4. yaa	11. dam	18. dtalaat
5. dtaa	12. saa	19. yaak
6. dtaai	13. yaak	20. k(h)aao
7. yaak	14. daao	

B.

1. ດາວ	6. ຍາກ	11. ທາກ
2. ລາວ	7. ຖາມ	12. ຂາວ
3. ງາມ	8. ຢາ	13. ບ້ຳ
4. ຈະ	9. ບ້ຳ	14. ລາວ
5. ຢາກ	10. ຢາກ	15. ຕະຫຼາດ

16. ດຳ   18. ຊາ   20. ຕາຍ
17. ປາ   19. ມາ

C.

1. ຈະ, ຊາ, ລາວ, ທາງ
2. ງາມ, ດາວ, ຕະຫຼາດ, ຕາ, ຍາ, ຍາກ
3. ຊາວ, ດາວ, ຕາ, ຕາຍ, ຖາມ, ນ້ຳ, ປາ, ຍາກ, ລາວ

Lesson 9

A.

1. Dao's medicine
2. Pretty fish
3. Dao is looking for tea.
4. (S)he vomited.
5. (S)he wants to come to the market.
6. Dao is coming.
7. White fish
8. (S)he will look for fish.

B.

1. ປາຊາວ
2. ດາວຊອກທາຍຢາ
3. ຍາກ
4. ລາວຣາກ
5. ປາຈະມາ
6. ຊາດາວ
7. ລາວງາມ
8. ປາຍາກຣາກ

Lesson 10

A.

1. **dii laai**
2. **gap**
3. **juhh**
4. **k(h)aw**
5. **mii**
6. **bpit**
7. **gin**
8. **hak**
9. **luhh**
10. **hok**
11. **baw**
12. **tammadaa**
13. **konlaao**
14. **luhhm**
15. **nyang**
16. **baw**
17. **t(h)uhhk**
18. **kuhhgan**
19. **nok**
20. **nyang**

B.

1.	ມີ	8.	ປິດ	15.	ຄືກັນ
2.	ລືມ	9.	ຂໍ	16.	ທຳມະດາ
3.	ຄືນ	10.	ຫິວ	17.	ຈຶ່
4.	ດີໝາຍ	11.	ຕຶກ	18.	ກັບ
5.	ບໍ່	12.	ຮັກ	19.	ຄືນລາວ
6.	ຍັງ, ທຍັງ	13.	ມິກ	20.	ບໍ່
7.	ຢາ	14.	ກິນ		

C.

1. ກັບ, ທຳມະດາ, ມິກ, ລືມ
2. ກັບ, ກິນ, ຂໍ, ຄືນລາວ, ຈຶ່, ບໍ່, ປິດ, ມີ
3. ກິນ, ຂໍ, ຄືກັນ, ຍັງ, ດີໝາຍ, ບໍ່, ຫຶ, ຮັກ

Lesson 11
A.

1. (S)he still has not returned to Lao.
2. Dao has a bird.
3. Lao people like to eat fish.
4. I forgot too.
5. The bird is going to look for fish.
6. Do you like it?
7. Dao has some very good medicine.

B.

1. ລາວມັກມິກຂາວ
2. ລາວມີບໍາຫຼາຍ
3. (ຂ້ອຍຈະ) ກັບຕະຫຼາດຄືກັນ
4. ເຈົ້າຮັກລາວບໍ່?
5. ລາວບໍ່ມີ
6. ຫາມລາວ
7. ຕະຫຼາດຍັງມີມິກງາມ, ປາຂາວ(ແລະ)ຍາດິ

Lesson 12

A.

1. gung	11. sawn	21. p(h)usaai
2. nguua	12. bawk	22. diao
3. supaap	13. suup	23. k(h)uaa
4. k(h)ian	14. jawk	24. k(h)awy
5. k(h)awng	15. kuaay	25. hawn
6. nawn	16. wiak	26. nawy
7. guaa	17. nyung	27. huu
8. hian	18. muu	28. p(h)uusaao
9. dtua	19. siang	
10. guaa	20. yut	

B.

1. ຜົວ	11. ຮູ້	21. ຂອຍ
2. ນອນ	12. ຄວາຍ	22. ຜູ້ຊາຍ
3. ກຸ້ງ	13. ຂອງ	23. ບອກ
4. ຈອກ	14. ຜູ້ສາວ	24. ຮຽນ
5. ຍຸດ	15. ຮ້ອນ	25. ຄ່ວ
6. ສູບ	16. ຍຸງ	26. ສຽງ
7. ສຸພາບ	17. ຕົວະ	27. ສອນ
8. ວິວ	18. ໝູ່	28. ນ້ອຍ
9. ວຽກ	19. ຂຽນ	
10. ຂວາ	20. ກ່ວາ	

C.

1. ຄວາຍ, ສຸພາບ, ຜູ້ສາວ, ຍຸດ

2. ກຸ້ງ, ຂອງ, ຈອກ, ດີກ່ວາ, ຄ່ວ, ຜູ້ສາວ, ວຽກ, ໝູ່

3. ວິວ, ສູບ, ສອນ, ຍຸງ, ບອກ, ຜົວ, ຮູ້, ຮຽນ

Lesson 13

A.

1. I know Dao's husband.
2. Lao person
3. Nawy studies a lot.
4. It's very hot.
5. Nawy is looking for cigarettes.
6. Do you have it?
7. I don't have any.
8. I have a lot of work (to do).

B.

1. ຄົນດງວ
2. ຂ້ອຍບໍ່ສູບຢາ
3. ຢຸດ!
4. ຍັງບໍ່ຮູ້ບໍ?
5. ຜົວຂອງຜູ່ຂ້ອຍກັນຄວາຍຂອງຂ້ອຍ
6. ຖາມນ້ອຍຮູ້ນັກບໍ?
7. ລາວຕິອະທຫງາຍ
8. ຍຸງນ້ອຍກ່ວານິກຂາວ
9. ກິນກຸ້ງບໍ?
10. ຜູ້ຍິງຂຽນດິກວ່າຜູ້ຊາຍ

Lesson 14

A.

1. weei laa
2. saaep
3. jai
4. nawn
5. luhhm
6. k(h)aaeng haaeng
7. bpai
8. gai
9. daaeng
10. joon
11. mii
12. wai
13. kuhh gan
14. doo laa
15. laaeo
16. poot
17. nyung
18. dtaaeng ngaan
19. laai
20. paaeng

B.

1. ຢານ້ອຍ
2. ໂຈນ
3. ໄຫ
4. ໂຊດາ
5. ຄົນລາວ
6. ເອລາ
7. ແຕກ
8. ໄມງ
9. ທຳມະດາ
10. ແຊບ
11. ໂພດ
12. ໄວ
13. ກຸ້ງ
14. ແຕ່ງງານ
15. ໃຈ
16. ໂຄລາ
17. ໂຮງໝໍ
18. ຢາກມາ
19. ໃບລິກ
20. ໝາກແຕງ

C.

1. ໄກ, ໃຈ, ໂຊກດີ, ຜູ້ສາວ, ໄວ
2. ແຊບ, ຕົວະ, ຜົວ, ໂພດ, ໝາກແຕງ, ຍາ, ໂຮງໝໍ
3. ກັບ, ຈິ່, ດີ, ແຕງ, ໄທ, ໃນ, ແພງ, ແລ້ວ, ເວລາ

Lesson 15

A.

1. Is it (delicious)?
2. Nawy is already married.
3. (S)he still doesn't have a boyfriend/girlfriend.
4. What time is it?
5. Can you go faster?
6. I don't have time.
7. What time are you going to school?
8. Cucumbers are really too expensive.

B.

1. ໂຊກດີ!
2. ຕະຫຼາດປິດຈັກໂມງ?
3. ສິບໂມງຂ້ອຍຈະໄປວຽກ
4. ພາສາລາວບໍ່ຍາກໂພດ
5. ຈອກ (ຂ້ອຍ) ແຕກແລ້ວ
6. ກິນແລ້ວ
7. ຜູ້ຊາຍແຂງແຮງຍາກແຕ່ງງານຜູ້ສາວງາມ
8. ຂຽນລາວໄດ້ບໍ?

Lesson 16

A.

1. bp(err)t	8. kuhh gan	15. ng'n
2. yen	9. jep	16. het
3. s(err)n	10. b(er)ng	17. pben
4. hai	11. k(err)'y	18. men
5. dek	12. p(h)et	19. k(er)ng
6. f(err)	13. kem	20. dtem
7. weei laa	14. laaeo	

B.

1.	ເງິນ	8.	ຂໍ
2.	ເຕັມ	9.	ເຮັດ
3.	ເໝັນ	10.	ເຄີຍ
4.	ເປີ	11.	ແພງໂພດ
5.	ເຂົ້ນ	12.	ເດັກ
6.	ນິກນ້ອຍ	13.	ເຢັນ
7.	ເຈັບ	14.	ເປັນ

15.	ເຜັດ
16.	ແຊບ
17.	ເຄີ່ງ
18.	ງາມຫຼາຍ
19.	ເບິ່ງ
20.	ໃນ

C.

1. ເຕັມ, ເດັກ, ເຕັມ, ເປັນ, ເວລາ, ໃຫ້
2. ເຄີ່ງ, ເຄີຍ, ຄິກັນ, ເງິນ, ເປີດ, ເຜັດ, ເປີ
3. ເຕັມ, ເງິນ, ເຈັບ, ເຂົ້ນ, ເດັກ, ເບິ່ງ, ເປັນ, ເຮັດ

Lesson 17

A.

1. Do you have cold (iced) tea?
2. Have you ever been to Thailand?
3. Ouch! (It hurts)
4. 2:30
5. I don't have a lot of money.
6. Is it too spicy?
7. What is the little kid doing?
8. Do you have time?

B.

1. ເປີເຜັດຫຼາຍ
2. ເບິ່ງລາວ
3. ປາເຕັມໂພດ
4. ເຄີຍໄປບໍ່?
5. ຍັງບໍ່ເຄີຍໄປ
6. ສາມໂມງເຄີ່ງມາບ້ານຂ້ອຍໄດ້ບໍ່?
7. ລາວເປັນຜູ້ຊາຍ
8. ແຊບບໍ່?

Lesson 18

A.

1.	lae	7.	ng'n	13.	siaa
2.	saw	8.	yaak	14.	so
3.	p(h)et	9.	dto	15.	biaa
4.	miaa	10.	nae nam	16.	nyung
5.	paw waa	11.	dte	17.	s(err)n
6.	naw	12.	jawk		

B.

1. ແລະ	6. ໂຕະ	11. ເຂີນ
2. ໂຂະ	7. ຍຸງ	12. ເນາະ
3. ເຕະ	8. ເພາະວ່າ	13. ຈອກ
4. ແນະນຳ	9. ເງິນ	14. ຍາກ
5. ເມຍ	10. ເສຍ	15. ໂຂະ

C.

1. ເຕະ, ໂຕະ, ເພາະວ່າ, ຍາກ
2. ໂຂະ, ແນະນຳ, ເນາະ, ເຜັດ, ແລະ
3. ກິນ, ເສຍ, ໂຂະ, ຍຸງ, ແນະນຳ, ຍາກ

Lessons 19–23

Lesson 19

A.

1. Introduce my friend.
2. Eat fish because it's delicious.
3. Dao and Nawy have been to Lao.
4. Very expensive, huh.
5. Get out of here!
6. His mistress smokes a lot.
7. What is (s)he eating?
8. Nok lost his wife's water buffalo.

B.

1. ຍາກຫຼາຍເນາະ?
2. ລາວເຄີຍກິນເຜິບ່?
3. ຂ້ອຍບໍ່ມີເງິນເພາະວ່າຂ້ອຍກິນຫຼາຍໆ
4. ຮ້ອນເນາະ?
5. ມັກໂຕະຂ້ອຍບໍ່?
6. ເຜັດໂພດເນາະ
7. ຜົວຂອງຜູ້ຂ້ອຍເສຍຄວາຍຂອງຂ້ອຍ

Lesson 20

A.

1. jow
2. huhh'a
3. hian
4. muhh'ai
5. huhh'an
6. t(h)ow
7. tuhh'a naa
8. kuhh'ang
9. bpit
10. mow
11. lae
12. dtaaeng ngaan
13. duhh'an
14. ow
15. luhh'at
16. muhh'ang
17. bow
18. wow
19. muhh'ak
20. het

B.

1. ເດືອນ
2. ເວົ້າ
3. ເຮືອນ
4. ຂາວ
5. ເຮັດ
6. ເຈົ້າ
7. ເຕົ້າ
8. ເຮົາ
9. ເບາະ
10. ເລືອດ
11. ເຮືອ
12. ເຄືອງ
13. ດາວ
14. ແຂບ
15. ເມິງາ
16. ເມື່ອຍ
17. ເມືອກ
18. ເມືອງ
19. ເບິງາ
20. ເທິ່ອໜ້າ

C.

1. ເຈົ້າ, ເບິງາ, ປິດ, ເມືອງ, ເລືອດ
2. ເຕົ້າ, ເທິ່ອໜ້າ, ເມືອກ, ເມື່ອຍ, ແລະ, ເວົ້າ, ເຮົາ
3. ເຄືອງ, ເດືອນ, ເທິ່ອໜ້າ, ເບິງາ, ເມິງາ, ເລືອດ, ເຮັດ, ເຮືອ

Lesson 21

A.

1. Do you already have a girlfriend/boyfriend?
2. They are drunk already.
3. What did (s)he say?
4. Give it to me.

5. It's really humid, huh?
6. Do you want to go next month?
7. Are you tired?
8. Lao people like to say "Never mind (no problem)."

B.

1. ເຈົ້າບໍ່ກລາວແລ້ວບໍ່?
2. ເອົາເຜັ່ບໍ່ໃສ່ເລືອດ
3. ເຈົ້າຈິ່ຂ້ອຍໄດ້ບໍ່?
4. ເຈົ້າງາມຫຼາຍຄືກັນ
5. ຂໍສອງຈອກແດ່
6. ຄວາຍຄືກ່ວາງເຮືອດ
7. ເສຍຫຍັງ?
8. ເມົ່າແລ້ວບໍ່?

Lesson 23

A.

1. bpai
2. k(err)'y
3. baw
4. p(h)uu saai
5. naw
6. laao
7. ow
8. sook dii
9. tam ma daa
10. k(h)awng k(h)awy
11. nyung
12. mow
13. dtalaat
14. faaen
15. hian
16. f(err)
17. yaasuup
18. kondiao
19. het wiak
20. bpit
21. laaeo
22. p(h)uua
23. gin
24. dtaaeng ngaan
25. anggit
26. p(h)et
27. luhhm
28. maa
29. jow
30. nawy

Anggit (ອັງກິດ) means "English," as in **paasaa anggit** (the English language).

B.

1. ມີ	11. ງານຫຼາຍ	21. ຫຍູ່
2. ຮ້ອນ	12. ແຊບ	22. ເອົ້າ
3. ປາ	13. ໄດ້	23. ນ້ຳ
4. ບອກ	14. ຍັງ	24. ຮູ້
5. ກັບບ້ານ	15. ເກີນ	25. ເສຍ
6. ຜູ້ສາວ	16. ຍາກ	26. ມັກ
7. ຈີ່	17. ນອນ	27. ແພງໂພດ
8. ສິບໂມງເຄິ່ງ	18. ຍຸດ	28. ໄວ
9. ເໜື່ອຍ	19. ຄິທ່ວາ	29. ເວລາ
10. ເມຍ	20. ເປີດ	30. ໃຈ

C.

1. ແຊບ, ຍັງ, ຕະຫຼາດ, ບໍ່, ລາວ, ຮຽນ
2. ຫຍູ່, ຄິກັນ, ດາວ, ບອກ, ປາ, ຍາກ, ເມາະ, ເສຍ, ເອົ້າ
3. ກັບ, ຂ້ອຍ, ໃຈ, ເຈົ້າ, ແດງ, ນ້ຳ, ປິດ, ຜູ້ສາວ, ເຜ, ເມົາ, ຫຼາຍ

D.

1. ກິນແລ້ວບໍ່?	9. ບໍ່ມີເວລາ
2. ເໜື່ອຍຫຼາຍ	10. ຂ້ອຍຍາກກິນເຜັ ເຜັດ
3. ຈັກໂມງແລ້ວ?	11. ບອກລາວເຈົ້າບອກຂຍັງຂ້ອຍ
4. ເຈົ້າແຕ່ງງານແລ້ວບໍ່?	12. ຂ້ອຍເອົ້າພາສາລາວຍັງບໍ່ດີ
5. ແຊບຫຼາຍ	13. ສູບຍາບໍ່?
6. ຮ້ອນຫຼາຍເມາະ?	14. ຂ້ອຍຈະໄປນອນ
7. ເຈົ້າເຄີຍໄປປະເທດໄທບໍ່?	15. ເຈົ້າບໍ່ຈິ້ຂ້ອຍບໍ່?
8. ໄປໄວທ່ວາໄດ້ບໍ່?	

E.

1. I'm going back home at 2:30.
2. You are kind.
3. It's hot, huh?
4. My friend likes to sleep a lot.
5. Too expensive, huh.

6. What does your husband do?
7. Are you already drunk?
8. Is it delicious?
9. He speaks Lao (language) better than me.
10. Please ask him/her.
11. Bring the money.
12. Does (s)he have a boyfriend/girlfriend already?
13. I've never eaten mosquitoes.
14. My friend's wife knows Nok's friend's husband.
15. Have you already eaten?

NOTE

Practice your Lao with the included MP3 audio files!

This CD contains <u>MP3 audio files</u>.

You can play MP3 files on your computer (most computers include a default MP3 player); in your portable MP3 player; on many mobile phones and PDAs; and on some newer CD and DVD players.

You can also convert the MP3 files and create a regular audio CD, using software and a CD writing drive.

To play your MP3 files:

1. Open the CD on your computer.
2. Click on the MP3 file that you wish to play, to open it. The file should start playing automatically. *(If it doesn't, then perhaps your computer does not have an MP3 player; you will need to download one. There are dozens of players available online, and most of them are free or shareware. You can type "mp3 player" or "music downloads" into your search engine to find some.)*